That just about Baux-ite's:
The possible 15 year Bauxite boom in Australia

Contents

1.   Introduction

2.   Subjects/Themes

- Bauxite Boom
- What is Bauxite?
- Bauxite compared to other resources
- Bauxite mining process
- Countries who deal in Bauxite/Competition of Bauxite
- Mining money-people (millionaires and billionaires)
- Chinese market for Bauxite
- Australian market for Bauxite
- Climate Change-Environmental issues

1. Introduction

There was the Coal mining boom...then along came the Bauxite juggernaut.

It can be said, Australia, compared to other areas around the world, is full of rich, quality resources, like Bauxite.

It would be interesting to know, is Bauxite a recent phenomenon, or has it been there all along, and relevant groups, were ignorant or just mislead as to what to do about it.

One thing is for sure, China is definitely at the basis for a sudden interest in Bauxite.

2. Subjects/Themes

Bauxite Boom

Australian Bauxite Limited states, how the demand rate for Bauxite is growing faster than global industrial production can supply. Local construction-resource group, Rio Tinto, disclosed they are set to benefit, "15 year Bauxite export boom", especially with a recent 'Chinese-Australian Free Trade Agreement' (Stringer, D. June 2, 2016). Rio Tinto are said to have committed an almighty, "$US 9 million ($AUS 2.6 billion)", to take advantage of this fantastic opportunity. Stringer states, to note the strength of aluminium, "aluminium is one of the fastest-growing metals, in the medium-to-long term. Australian exports in general are looking to rise, "an average of 36 % a year, from 2018 to 2021," according to the Department of Industry, Innovation and Science. These statistics are a turnaround for Aluminium in Australia with a 3.3% increase in 2015, following a decline in 2014, progressing since 2008.

China will use the Bauxite to channel its "aluminium smelters and alumina refineries". China has increased its annual imports, from 2.2 million tons to a whopping 50 million tons, over the past ten years.

What is Bauxite?

According to Stringer, "Bauxite is a mined raw material that is processed into alumina, and intermediate product, that is further refined into aluminium." Aluminium compounds are derived from Bauxite. Wikipedia states, "Bauxite is an aluminium ore, and is the world's main source of aluminium." A French chemist, Henri Sainte-Claire Deville, named the mineral, 'Bauxite'.

Australia is noteworthy for producing high quality Bauxite. Chief Executive of Metallica Minerals, Simon Slesarewich, states, "...our bauxite is very good quality...it comes down to quality...it depends on things like the levels of actual bauxite in the ore and other deleterious minerals present (McHugh, B. March 29, 2016)." The top quality of Australian Bauxite was one of the reasons why China selected Australia as one of its suppliers. So Australia, has among the world's largest deposits of Bauxite, but also some of the best quality Bauxite-Ore(McHugh, B. March 29, 2016). 'Recycle Nation' states how there is enough Bauxite globally, to last at least another 400 years. Australian Bauxite "meets close to one-third of our total global demand" (Recycle Nation)

Bauxite compared to other resources

With bauxite mining, other resources are uncovered and or effected, with "combustion by-products, caustic aerosols, dust from bauxite, limestone, charred lime, alumina and sodium salt." (Recycle Nation) According to Australian Mining, 'Iron Ore' currently has the most production, with 443,200 tonnes; Bauxite has 68,000, 000 tonnes; Coal has 227,900,00 tonnes; Copper has 880,000 tonnes; Gold 275.5 tonnes; and Zinc 1,508,000 tonnes.

There is an ever-decreasing export of various minerals from China, including gold, silver, and rare metals. Bauxite, on the contrary is being increased for China's alumina-aluminium needs. Chinese-owned company, 'Xinfa Aurum Exploration' was granted the first bauxite mine from the Fijian Government, on the second Fijian island of Vanua Levu. This mine will look to earn Fiji, 20 million Fiji dollars (11.11 million US dollars) – (Alpha Axiom).

Bauxite mining process

Bauxite is relatively easy to mine because it is "almost always found near the surface of relevant terrain, causing less burden."

'Recycle Nation' calls it 'open-pit mining', "where large swaths of earth are excavated relatively close to the surface in order to remove valuable materials, enabling workers to locate raw bauxite." Wikipedia states, how "from 2010, approximately 70% to 80-85% of the world's dry Bauxite is processed first into alumina, and then into aluminium by electrolysis." However, there are environmental concerns using electrolysis for aluminium production. The left-over 10% goes to non-metal uses, and remainder put to Bauxite-type applications like abrasives and refractories (Australian Bauxite Limited).

A positive of bauxite mining, is that, "aluminium is infinitely and economically recyclable, losing none of its integrity, even when it is melted down repeatedly"...This recycling earns money for municipalities, charities and community causes (Recycle Nation). A negative of bauxite mining, according to 'Recycle Nation', is that "all native vegetation in the mining region is removed, resulting in a loss of habitat and food for local wildlife and soil erosion." However, large numbers of aluminium beverage cans end up being put in landfills around the world, taking even up to 500 years to be recycled. A proper recycling process can save these precious landfills and stop waste of materials produced (Recycle Nation).

Countries who deal in Bauxite/Competition of Bauxite

According to Aluminium for Future Generations (ALU) "around 50km2 is newly mined for bauxite globally every year, or around one square metre distributed per tonne of aluminium produced." Bauxite, in fact, carbonate bauxite, is predominantly found in Europe and Jamaica, the tropics and

Australia. Wikipedia states, how in 2010, Australia was second to Guinea in the world's production of Bauxite, with Vietnam, Jamaica, Brazil, India, and further on, China to follow on. Australian Bauxite Limited states, how emerging economies, Asia and India, have a particular strong demand for Bauxite. The world's supply of Bauxite are sufficient to meet demand standards worldwide, for many centuries to come, or about 400 years as first planned for.

The Bauxite market is undergoing significant structural change. There has traditionally been an integrated bauxite-alumina-aluminium industry in Australia. However, the Chinese alumina industry is on the rise, together with changes in Indonesia creating new market opportunities for direct export of the raw commodity. Indonesia is the largest exporter of bauxite in the world, but like China, is concentrating on furthering its own bauxite-alumina-aluminium industry (Geoscience Australia). With Indonesia usually exporting bauxite to China, other bauxite mining, like in Australia and Africa, will make up any shortfall. ABC News states how Australian mining needs to properly manage and maintain its low costs of production, fluctuations in the mining sector and how workforces are regulated, especially with shifts in mining investment and workers being laid off, for example, at sites across the Upper Hunter (March 11, 2013).

Mining money-people (millionaires and billionaires)

News.com.au has disclosed how, the new rich are blue-collar people, with tradies, miners and construction workers. Hospitality, arts and retail are in the bottom three of wealth earned in Australia (May 3, 2012).

There are some popular and influential Mining millionaires and billionaires in Australia, who are very public figures in the media, with Gina Rinehardt, Clive Palmer and young Nathan Tinkler, to name a few. Other notable Australian mining entrepreneurs are Claude de Bernales, Rick Stowe, Alan Bond, Robert Champion de Crespigny, Stan Perron, Joseph Gutnick, Lang Hancock, Andrew Forrest, Peter Wright, Mark Creasy (Australian Mining Entrepreneurs, Wikipedia).

Gina Rinehart is Australia's second richest person, with $8.5 billion in 2016, $0.3 billion behind first runner, Blair Parry-Okeden, with $8.8 billion (Forbes.com.au). Mining money-people have been negatively affected by a downturn in mining, with Gina Rinehart's wealth dropping from $30 billion in 2012, to

$11 billion in 2015, to $8.5 million in 2016 (Kruger, C. April 18, 2015).

A current poorer price for iron ore, as well as other factors affecting mining, have had some mining money people be affected. Clive Palmer has his iron ore, nikel and coal holdings, having some current troubles with his nikel businesses. Palmer was a temporary independent Australian Government politician, voted in previously under the Palmer party. Palmer recently stepped down as a politician, succumbing to the political and media pressure (Clive Palmer, Wikipedia). Andrew Forrest' wealth was $13 billion in 2008, and currently possibly only $500 million (Kruger, C. April 18, 2015). Nathan Tinkler is a former mining magnate and one of Australia's youngest billionaires, and is apparently nearing possible bankruptcy. Wikipedia discloses that Tinkler's wealth in 2013 was a merely $235 million (Nathan Tinkler, Wikipedia).

Chinese market for Bauxite

There has been an aggressive expansion in Chinese Bauxite-Aluminium refining capacity. Australian Bauxite Limited (ABL) highlights, the reason for such a pull of Bauxite-Aluminium is the "shortage of bauxite deposits in China, and the higher cost of treating the difficult Chinese domestic bauxite." China is buying mines and mining shares, for example the Yankuang Corporation is designing and constructing a modern refinery in southwest Western Australia. Yankuang, for instance, owns 88% of Yanzhou Coal, which bought 'Australia's Felix Resources' (Alpha Axiom). Bauxite exporting to China has endured a tightening of Chinese government policies and regulations on mining. Examples of this are China expecting exporting-importing mining companies, to "demonstrate a possession of a licence, an environmental permit from the local Chinese government and social securities for workers (Alpha Axiom)."

Indonesia was previously a long-term supplier of Bauxite to China, but is now lacking in amounts remaining of Bauxite to mine and export. Indonesia bauxite imports fell to just over 65% in 2007, from approximately 90% in 2006 (Alpha Axiom). Indonesia, recently, even banned its own exports of Bauxite in early 2014 (McHugh, B. March 29, 2016). Malaysia was a competitor of Australia, "immediately taking advantage of the Indonesian ban, and started mining and exporting large amounts of Bauxite to China, before Australia got a look it. This establishes a fantastic opportunity, at least at first analysed, for Australia to capitalise on exported Bauxite.

Australian market for Bauxite

Geoscience Australia states, how Australia "represented 30% of global production in 2012, and 80% of production exported". Geoscience Australia state, "Australia was the leading producer of bauxite globally in 2012, the second largest producer of alumina and the fifth largest producer of aluminium." Australian Bauxite Limited (ABL) highlighted how the industry for Bauxite-Aluminium in Australia is a large combination of industries of mining, refining, smelting and semi-fabrication. Such industries are very important economically, nationally and globally. The lines of Bauxite employment are shown with "transport, packaging, building and construction," to provide much of the demand for the metal in Australia (ABL). Stringer states how 'motor vehicles' are likely to satisfy about half of the demand of Australian Bauxite-Aluminium exports.

ABL continues, by showing how, in Australia, there are five bauxite mining operations, seven alumina refineries, six primary aluminium smelters, twelve extrusion plants and two rolled product (sheet, plate and foil) mills.

Geoscience Australia breaks the industry down even further, with five long-term bauxite mines at Weipa, Gove, Huntly, Boddington and Willowdale; seven alumina refineries at Gove, Yarwun; QAL, Kwinana, Pinjarra; Wagerup and Worsley. Five primary aluminium smelters at Bell Bay, Boyne Island, Tomago, Portland and Point Henry; twelve extrusion mills in NSW, Victoria, South Australia, Qld and WA; and two rolled product plants, producing aluminium sheet, plate and foil in Victoria.

There are a number of large multinational mining companies in Australia, including <u>BHP Billiton</u>, <u>Newcrest</u>, <u>Rio Tinto</u>, <u>Alcoa</u>, <u>Chalco</u>, <u>Shenhua</u> (a Chinese mining company), <u>Alcan</u> and <u>Xstrata</u> operate in Australia (Mining in Australia, Wikipedia). To give an example, BHP is eyeing a Pilbara iron ore mine, in Western Australia (Evans, N. June 9, 2016). Also in Western Australia, and according to National Australia Bank research, the mining industry is looking to shed a mammoth 50,000 jobs (William, P. June 11, 2016). Australian Bauxite-specific companies aiming to capitalise on this Bauxite demand, are Australian Bauxite Limited, Bauxite Resources Limited, Gulf Alumina Limited, Aluminium for Future Generations and Metallica Minerals.

Climate Change-Environmental issues

A major problem with Bauxite and Aluminium, is the polluting emissions they produce, relating to climate change and being environmentally friendly. A large supply of electricity is required to produce aluminium. 'Recycle Nation' support this, stating how large amounts of electricity, water, coal and resources are required to transform raw bauxite into aluminium. Turnip, under Stringer, states, how "the production of aluminium shoots off 4 tonnes of carbon dioxide per tonne of aluminium into the air, and 200 million tonnes of carbon dioxide globally (June 2, 2016)." 'Recycle Nation' make a strong comment how smelters, with coal and aluminium, are "one of the most notoriously polluting fuel sources known to mankind." Recycle Nation states how the aluminium smelting process, "are 9,200 times more harmful than carbon dioxide and the effect on global warming." On a positive note, The Dirt, highlights how Australia has a reputation for 'greener mining', more than most nations, especially for a heavily environmentally regulated industry (The Dirt, April 24, 2013).

Turnip goes onto state, how the aluminium production process involves an electricity graphite electrolysis that pollutes. This problem relates to the suggestion and recommendation by Turnip, under Stringer, for more proper and advanced renewable energy products and services (June 2, 2016). Other examples, to name a few, are Ethanol-based unleaded petrol, recycling bins at home and work, electric motor vehicles, solar panels, wind farms and now scientists changing Co_2 into stone to combat climate change (AFP, June 10, 2016). 'Recycle Nation' discloses the products made with aluminium, for example, laundry detergent, cement, aspirin, roofing, soda cans, house siding, spark plugs, foil containers, foil wrap, makeup, appliances, etc.

Aluminium for Future Generations (ALU) states, on an environmental level, "80% of mines in 2008 are ISO 14001 certified by the International Aluminium Institute. Mining stakeholders are acknowledged, with traditional owners, landowners, government agencies and regulators, local communities and NGO's. An 87% of mines are monitored, reported and analysed. Over 80% of mines maintain an environmental awareness and training program for all employees and contractors.

Benefits of Mining in general/Politics and Governmental intervention and influence

The activities of mining companies can have positive and negative issues and consequences. In political circles, there are certain politicians, lobby groups and environmental and green groups, who would class the mining industry as having little benefits. An example of this is mentioned by The Dirt, where mining is viewed as "being keen to simply tear up the land, clear cut forest, extract all the minerals and basically salt the earth out of spite that nothing will ever grow again" (April 24, 2013).

The Dirt, classes mining, even primary industries, and government, as a 'love-hate relationship', where the government like the money from mining, but dislike the industry (April 24, 2013). There are issues of mine site rehabilitation and its financial guarantees, information related to the mining sector, a mining strategy incorporating principles of sustainable-environmental development and mining rights (Harvey, Y. August 2009).

Despite some governmental issues of tax and royalty issues, and putting profit over production, Harvey highlights some benefits of mining, with, "job creation, commercial international relationships, fiscal revenues, duties and taxes, community organisation, etc (Harvey, Y. August 2009). There are "metals and minerals that our society needs, for agriculture, housing, music, telecommunications, the environmental industry, construction, space exploration, medicine and leisure." (Harvey, Y. August 2009) Harvey states how some people and groups, have, "poor knowledge of the mining sector."

In short, Harvey states, how the mining industry drives the local and regional economy, in Australia and overseas. Money is spent on purchasing goods and services, locally and regionally. Examples of money spent, are, transport, environmental quality initiatives, salaries, levies, income taxes and social benefit programs and donations to community activities, training centres, hospitals and community centres, and involving the Aboriginal people.

Mining contribution to Australian economy

Although still relatively strong, iron ore prices have weakened, eroding the money from mining money-people like Gina Rinehart and Nathan Tinkler (Business Daily, June 8, 2016). Australian Mining states how, "the minerals resources industry accounts for more than 6 percent of Australia's economy, has 54% of Australia's total goods and services, and has invested more than $125 billion in Australia in the last 10 years. The mining industry's contribution to the Australian economy is now $121 billion a year." IbisWorld (April 2016) states, how Bauxite is expected to account for over one-third of global output in 2015-16. There has been an 11.7% increase in Bauxite mining, from 2011 to 2016, with $2 billion profit earned. Bauxite production in Australia is estimated to reach 83.5 million tonnes in 2015-16, up from 67.3 million tonnes in 2010-11.

3.   Bibliography

- ABC News (March 11, 2013) 'Competition forces mines to re-think costs'
- AFP (June 10, 2016) ' Scientists turn CO2 into stone to fight climate change'
- Alpha-Axiom, 'The Chinese Demand for Bauxite'
- Aluminium for Future Generations (ALU) 'Almost 80% of the mines surveyed in 2008 by the International Aluminium Institute are ISO 14001 certified'
- Australian Bauxite Limited, 'Market and Industry overview'
- Australian Mining, 'Australia's mineral wealth'
- 'Australian Mining Entrepreneurs', Wikipedia
- Babs, McHugh (March 29, 2016) 'Bauxite price slowly climbing, with tight global

supply and high demand from Chinese alumina refineries', ABC Rural
- Bauxite Resources Limited, 'Company Profile'
- 'Bauxite', <u>Wikipedia</u>
- Business Daily (June 8, 2016) 'Weak ore price hits Gina's bottom line,' <u>The Daily Telegraph</u>
- CIM.org (August 2009) 'Benefits of the Mining industry'
- 'Clive Palmer', <u>Wikipedia</u>
- Evans, Nick (June 9, 2016) 'BHP eyes massive Pilbara mine', <u>The West Australian</u>
- Forbes.com, 'Australia's 50 richest people'
- Geoscience Australia, 'Bauxite'
- IbisWorld (April 2016) 'Bauxite Mining in Australia: Market Research Report'
- 'Mining in Australia', <u>Wikipedia</u>
- 'Nathan Tinkler', <u>Wikipedia</u>

- News.com.au (May 3, 2012) 'New rich are Australia's tradies, miners and construction workers.'
- NSW Mining, 'Millionaires and Billionaires campaign against working families of the Hunter'
- Recycle Nation, 'What Aluminium extraction really does to the environment'
- Stringer, David (June 2, 2016) 'China demand to drive 15-year long Bauxite boom, says Rio Tinto', Sydney Morning Herald
- The Dirt (April 24, 2013) 'The benefits and burdens', Australian Mining
- Williams, Peter (June 11, 2016) ' More jobs to go in mining: NAB', The Western Australian